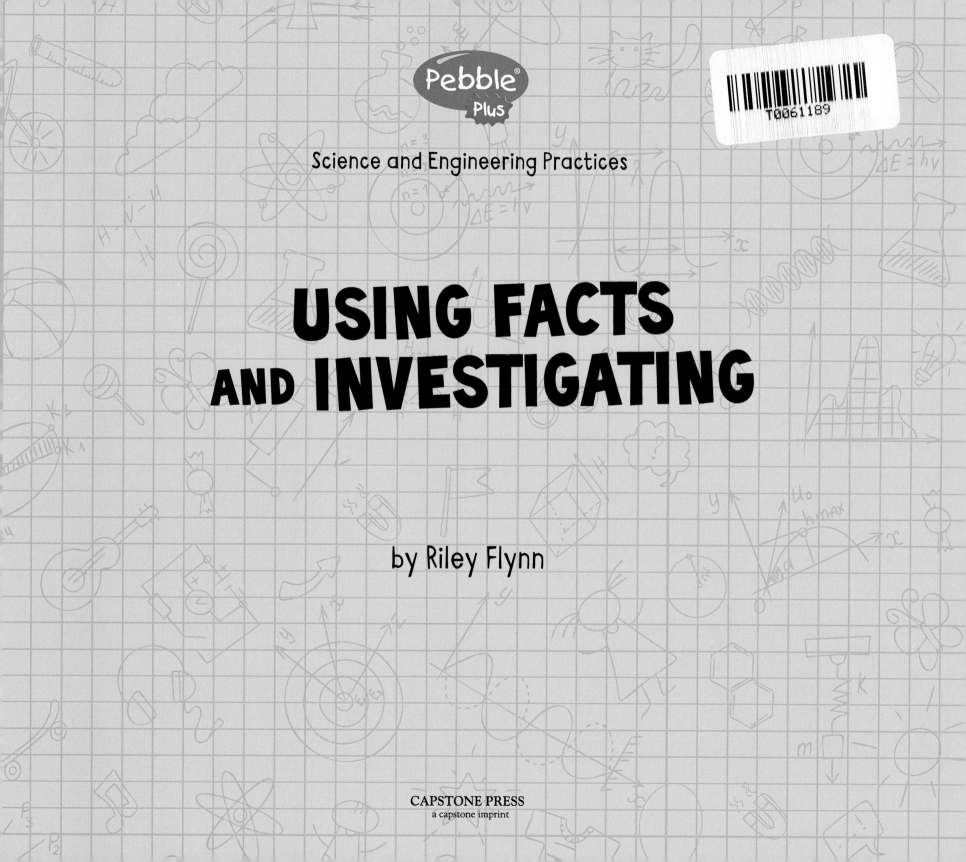

Pebble® Plus

Science and Engineering Practices

USING FACTS AND INVESTIGATING

by Riley Flynn

CAPSTONE PRESS
a capstone imprint

Pebble Plus is published by Capstone Press,
1710 Roe Crest Drive, North Mankato, Minnesota 56003
www.mycapstone.com

Library of Congress Cataloging-in-Publication Data
Cataloging-in-Publication data is on file with the Library of Congress.
ISBN 978-1-5157-0949-7 (library binding)
ISBN 978-1-5157-0981-7 (paperback)
ISBN 978-1-5157-1116-2 (eBook PDF)

Editorial Credits
Anna Butzer, editor; Sarah Bennett, designer; Eric Gohl, media researcher; Laura Manthe, production specialist

Photo Credits
iStockphoto: Christopher Futcher, 11, Gertjan_Ketelaars, 7, Marilyn Nieves, 9, Nicolefoto, 17; Shutterstock:
ffolas, 15, Lehrer, 5, parinyabinsuk, cover, Trofimov Denis, 13, wavebreakmedia, 19, Yuri Samsonov, 20

Design Elements: Shutterstock

Note to Parents and Teachers

The Science and Engineering Practices set supports Next Generation Science Standards
related to Science and Engineering Practices. This book describes and illustrates finding
information and making arguments. The images support early readers in understanding the
text. The repetition of words and phrases helps early readers learn new words. This book
also introduces early readers to subject-specific vocabulary words, which are defined in the
Glossary section. Early readers may need assistance to read some words and to use the
Table of Contents, Glossary, Read More, Internet Sites, Critical Thinking Using the Common
Core, and Index sections of the book.

Printed and bound in the USA.
001126

Table of Contents

What Are Facts?

You need to write a report on honeybees. How are you going to do it? You need to gather facts and conduct an investigation.

What is a fact? A fact is a piece of information that is true and accurate. Bees live in hives. They have six legs. These are facts.

What Is an Investigation?

An investigation is like a test.

It looks for answers to a question.

An investigation can solve a problem.

An engineer uses investigations to test designs. A scientist uses investigations to answer questions. You can conduct investigations like a scientist to gather facts.

Facts from Experiments

Let's experiment! An experiment is an investigation that can help you learn facts. Think of a question. What attracts bees?

You predict that sweet things attract bees. Put water in two bowls. Add sugar to one bowl. You observe that bees like the sweet water. You have a new fact!

Let's Investigate

Which spilled liquid will dry faster?
Make a prediction. Then find out!

What You Need:

- 1/4 cup (60 milliliters) water
- 1/4 cup (60 mL) apple juice
- 1/4 cup (60 mL) soda
- sidewalk chalk
- timer, clock, or watch

What You Do:

1. Find a sunny spot on a sidewalk or driveway.

2. Pour each liquid on the sidewalk or driveway. Be sure to leave space between each liquid.

3. Draw a circle around the edges of each spilled liquid. Write the liquid's name below the circle.

4. Observe the results. How long did it take each liquid to dry? Write the time in minutes.

5. Which liquid dried, or evaporated, first?

What Do You Think?

Make a claim. A claim is something you believe to be true. Why do you think one liquid dried faster than the others?

Glossary

engineer—a person who uses science and math to plan, design, or build

experiment—a scientific test to find out how something works

gather—to collect things

investigate—to search for facts to solve a problem or answer a question

observe—to watch someone or something closely in order to learn something

predict—to say what you think will happen in the future

problem—something that causes trouble

review—to study or examine again

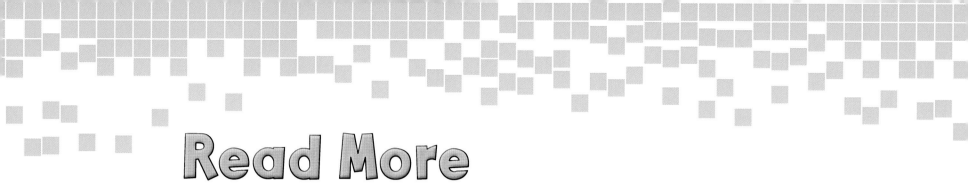

Read More

Rustad, Martha E.H. *Learning About Fact and Opinion.* Media Literacy for Kids. North Mankato, Minn.: Capstone Press, 2015.

Taylor-Butler, Christine. *Experiments with Liquids.* My Science Investigations. Chicago: Heinemann Library, 2012.

Internet Sites

FactHound offers a safe, fun way to find Internet sites related to this book. All of the sites on FactHound have been researched by our staff.

Here's all you do:
Visit www.facthound.com
Type in this code: 9781515709497

Check out projects, games and lots more at
www.capstonekids.com

Critical Thinking Using the Common Core

1. What is an investigation? (Key Ideas and Details)

2. Describe a time when you needed to gather facts to answer a question. (Integration of Knowledge and Ideas)

Index